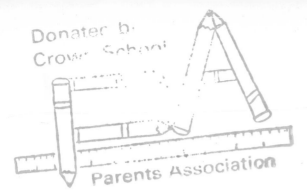

Donated by
Crow School

Parents Association

Acknowledgements

Illustrations by Steve Cox
Photographs by Zul Mukhida except for:
pp. 10, 11t, 19tr, 19bl, 25b Jenny Matthews; p. 11b Popperfoto;
pp. 18t, 19br Chris Fairclough; p. 26t E. T. Archive; p. 26b
Sir Ranulph Fiennes, Royal Geographical Society.

The author and publisher would like to thank the staff and pupils
of Patcham Infant School, Brighton.

A CIP catalogue record for this book is available
from the British Library.

ISBN 0-7136-3762-5

First published 1994 by A & C Black (Publishers) Ltd
35 Bedford Row, London WC1R 4JH

© 1994 A & C Black (Publishers) Ltd

Typeset by Rowland Phototypesetting Ltd, Bury St Edmunds, Suffolk
Printed in Belgium by Proost International Book Production.

going
places

People on the move

Barbara Taylor

Illustrations by Steve Cox

Photographs by Zul Mukhida and Jenny Matthews

Contents

A & C Black · London

Going on a journey

Do you know the way to school? How do you get there?
Do you walk, or go by bus or car? How long does it take?

When you travel from one place
to another, you are going on a
journey. Going to school is a
journey. Some journeys are short;
you don't need to go far to post a
letter. Other journeys are much
longer. Have you ever been on
a journey to another country?

Before you go on a journey, what sort of questions do you need to ask? You might want to find out how long the journey will take or what type of transport you will be using. Here are some other ideas.

Why go on journeys?

What sort of journeys have you been on this week? Have you been to see a friend or take a book back to the library? Perhaps you've been on a special journey such as a holiday.

Ask your friends about the journeys they went on this week. Why did they go on their journeys?

We're going swimming.

I went to tea with Alice on Tuesday.

I'm going to school.

See if you can draw a chart like this one to show all the different journeys. Which was the most popular journey?

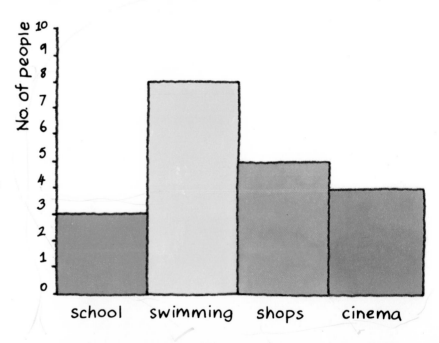

When people go on a journey, they often take things such as money or food with them. They might also collect things such as tickets during the journey.

Here are some pictures of things from four journeys. Can you guess where each person was going?

(The answers are at the bottom of the page.)

Journey 1

shopping list

purse

shopping basket

Journey 2

bus ticket

bunch of flowers

get-well card

Journey 3

balloon

party invitation

present

Journey 4

letter

front door key

Answers:

Journey 1 – going to the shops
Journey 2 – visiting someone in hospital
Journey 3 – going to a friend's party
Journey 4 – posting a letter

All over the world, people go on the same kinds of journeys. They might be going to school, visiting a friend or moving house. Most of the time people choose to make a journey, and can plan it before they go.

But some journeys, such as escaping from a flood, are a matter of life and death. These journeys have to be made in a hurry and people have to find the way as they go along.

Look carefully at these photographs. Can you work out why the people in each picture are going on a journey? Which of the journeys have been planned?

(The answers are at the bottom of the next page.)

1 Vietnam

2 England

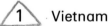

Mozambique

3

4 El Salvador

5 America

Answers:

5 To escape a flood
4 To find fresh grass for the animals
3 To run away from a war
2 To go on holiday
1 To go to work

How do you get there?

How do you get from place to place? Do you use the same kind of transport for each journey? The type of transport you use depends on how far you have to go and where you live.

Walking is a good way to cover short distances as long as the weather is fine and you haven't got too much to carry.

Trains are good for long journeys especially if you need to get somewhere quickly.

Cars and buses are useful for long and short journeys, but they sometimes get stuck in traffic jams.

Sometimes you might use several different kinds of transport in one journey.

Cycle to the station.

Take the train into town.

Walk to the office.

Ask an adult to help you find out more about the different types of transport in your local area.

Here are some of the things you could try to find out. What else can you think of?

Never stand near the road.

How many different types of transport can you spot?

How many cars, buses and lorries go past you in ten minutes?

How many vehicles are carrying goods such as food or machines?

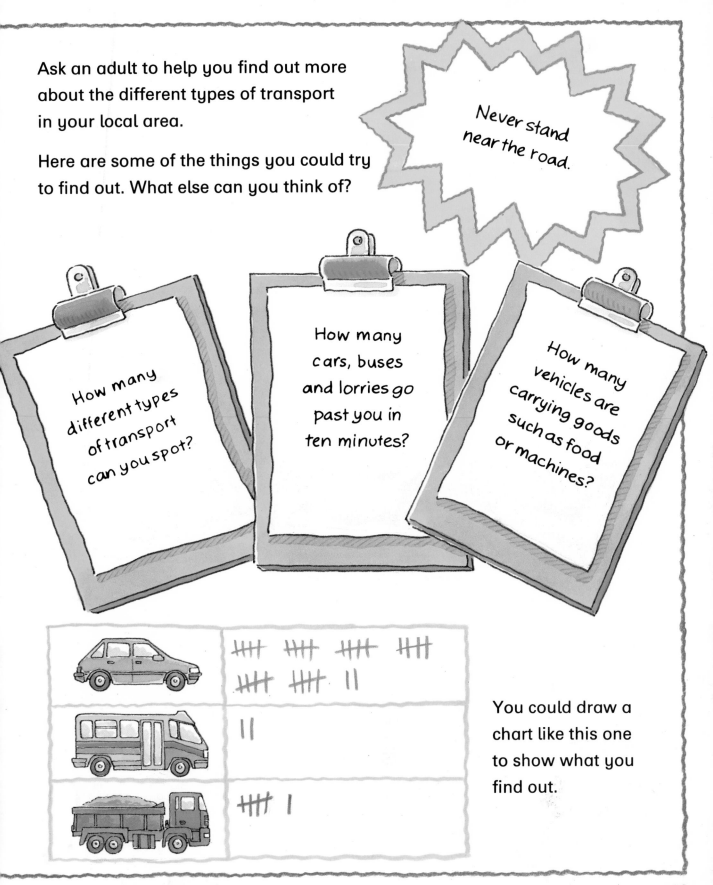

You could draw a chart like this one to show what you find out.

Planning a journey

Have you ever looked down at the ground from an aeroplane, or a really high building? This picture shows the countryside between Star City and Dragon Town as if you were looking down at the ground from high in the sky.

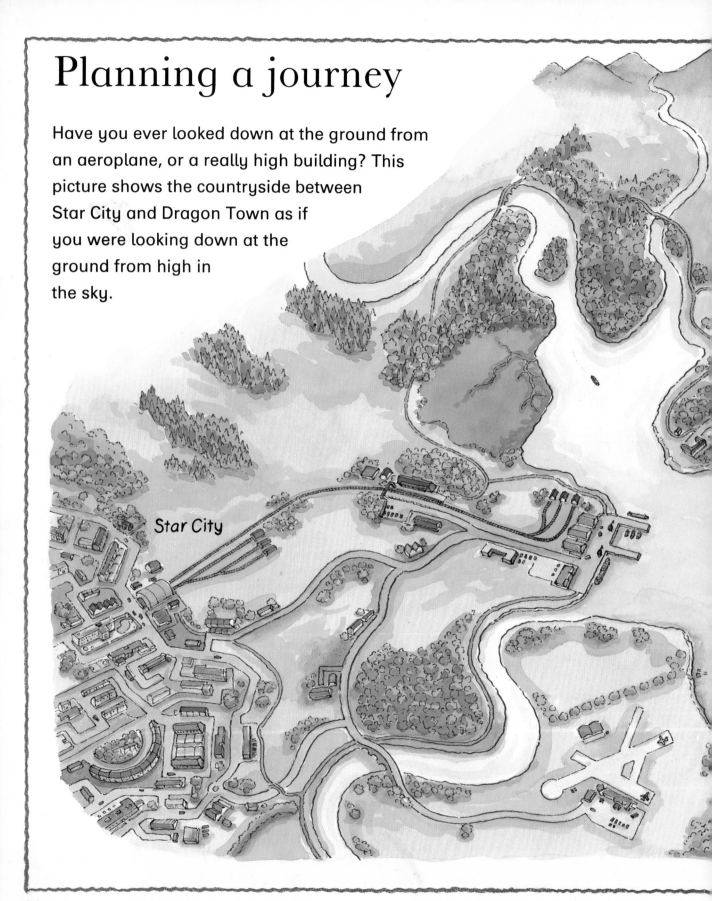

Star City

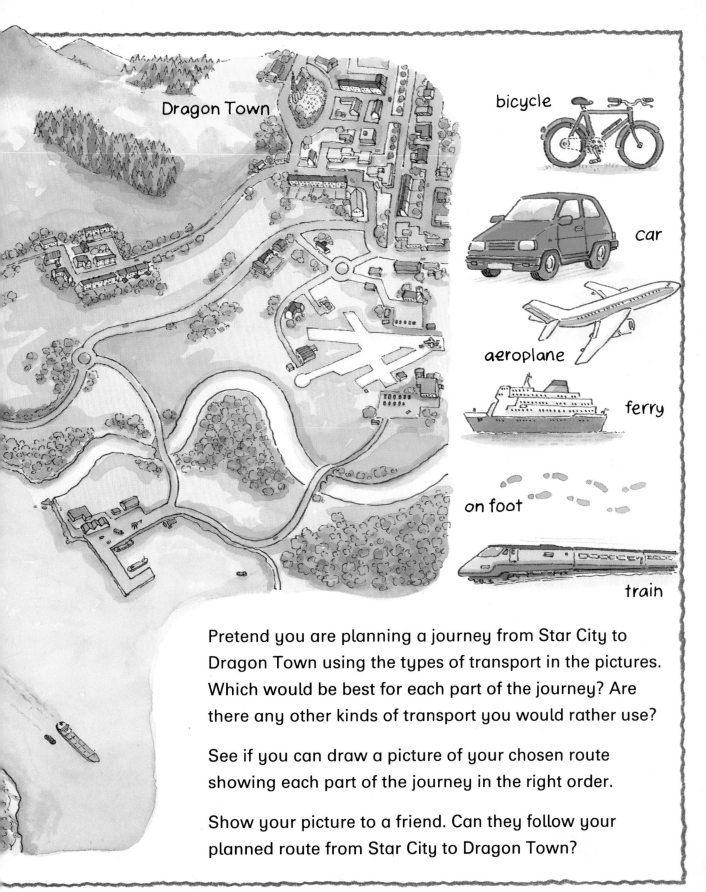

bicycle

car

aeroplane

ferry

on foot

train

Pretend you are planning a journey from Star City to Dragon Town using the types of transport in the pictures. Which would be best for each part of the journey? Are there any other kinds of transport you would rather use?

See if you can draw a picture of your chosen route showing each part of the journey in the right order.

Show your picture to a friend. Can they follow your planned route from Star City to Dragon Town?

Finding the way

This picture shows one way of getting from Star City to Dragon Town. The picture is called a map. How is it different from the picture on pages 14 and 15?

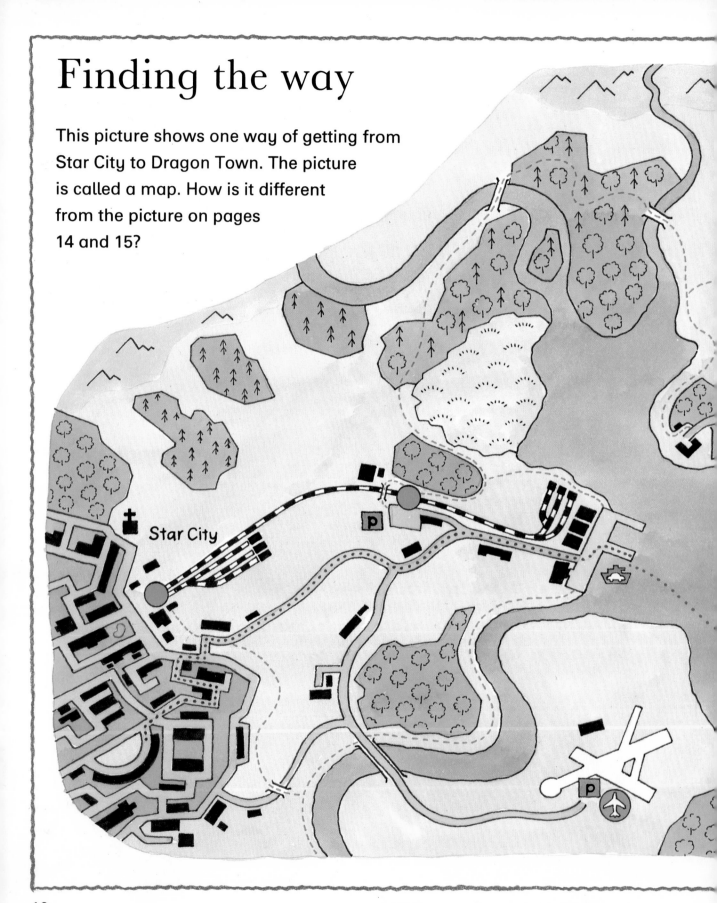

Star City

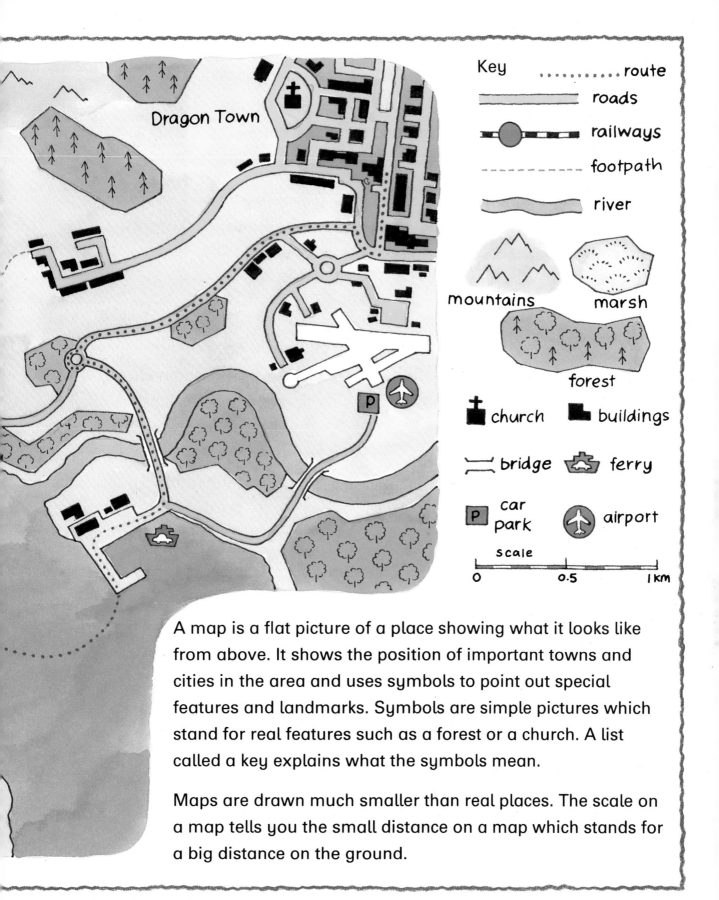

Key

.... route

roads

railways

footpath

river

mountains

marsh

forest

church   buildings

bridge   ferry

car park   airport

scale

0   0.5   1 km

A map is a flat picture of a place showing what it looks like from above. It shows the position of important towns and cities in the area and uses symbols to point out special features and landmarks. Symbols are simple pictures which stand for real features such as a forest or a church. A list called a key explains what the symbols mean.

Maps are drawn much smaller than real places. The scale on a map tells you the small distance on a map which stands for a big distance on the ground.

Try drawing a map of the journey from your home to your school. Close your eyes and think carefully about each part of the journey. Before you draw your map, try to describe the route out loud to a friend.

Try to fit your map on to a piece of paper the same size as this page. Draw symbols on your map to show where there are landmarks and add a key to explain what the symbols stand for.

Maps usually have an arrow pointing north so people can work out which direction to take. North is often at the top of a map and south is at the bottom. West is to the left and east is to the right. Is your school north, south, east or west of your home?

Ireland

How is your journey to school different from the ones in these pictures?

Sri Lanka

Uganda

Holland

Finding places

Maps help people to find places and to work out how long a journey is going to take. They show the best way of getting to a place and stop people getting lost on the way.

Here's a map of Rega 4 where Captain Veloz is being held prisoner by the evil Godor Wroth. The place is huge, but luckily she has managed to smuggle out a message telling you she is at 6B.

To find 6B, look at the lines crisscrossing the map. These are called grid lines and each one has a letter or a number. Put one finger on the end of line 6 and another finger on the end of line B. Slide your fingers along the lines until they meet at point 6B.

Can you find the entrance to the secret tunnel at 4D? What's hidden at 2E? Where is Godor Wroth's command headquarters?

Is Captain Veloz being held in the north, south, east or west?

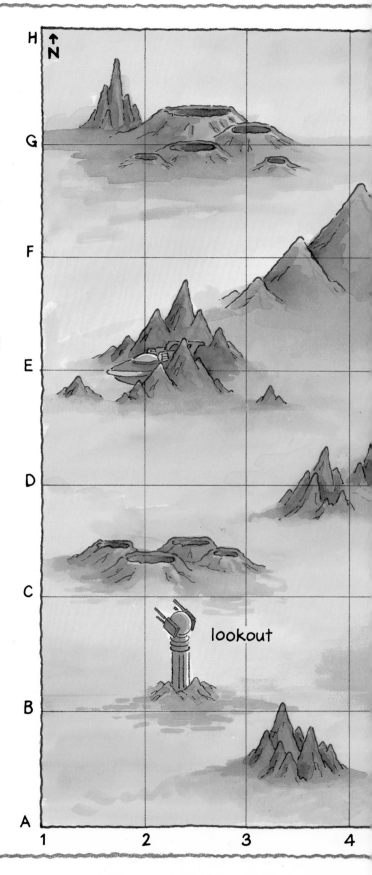

lookout

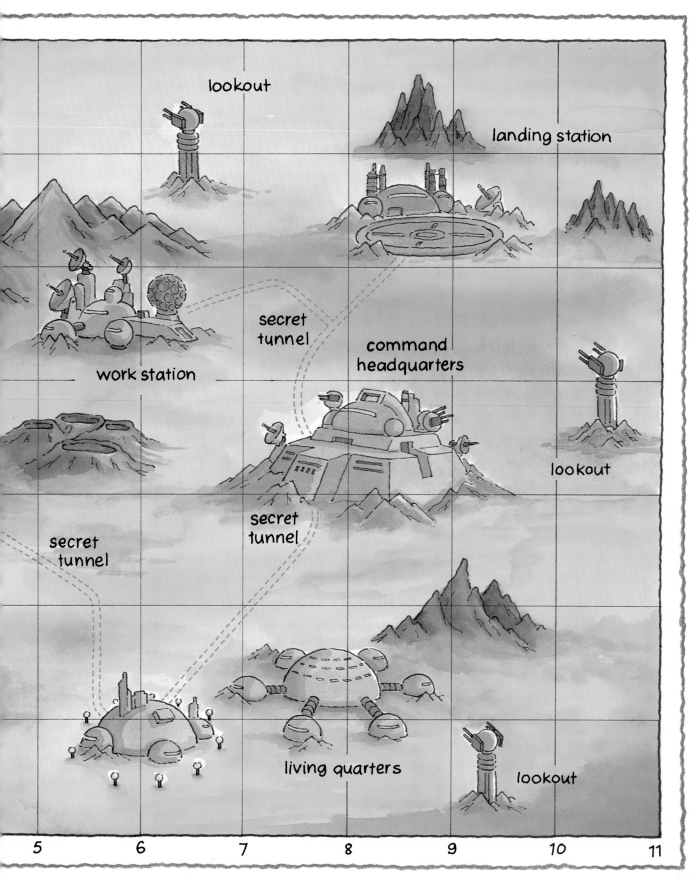

Town and country journeys

Do you live in a town or in the countryside? Here are some of the differences between journeys in the town and in the countryside. Which of these pictures reminds you of where you live?

busy roads

car fumes

lots of traffic

plenty of buses

peaceful

few buses

fresh air

empty roads

This girl went on a sound journey in her school playground. The school is in the middle of a big city. She had her eyes shut to help her listen to the sounds around her. These are some of the sounds she heard.

Can you think what sounds you might hear if you went on a sound journey in the country?

Green journeys

The journeys that we make can cause a lot of damage to the environment. Look out for these signs in your local area.

dirty air

holes in the road

litter

cracked pavement

How could we stop this damage? Should big lorries be kept out of city centres? Should there be more buses and trains so people could leave their cars at home? Should there be more space for bicycles on the roads?

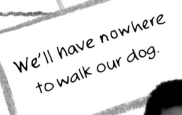

We'll have nowhere to walk our dog.

Imagine that a park near your home is going to be dug up to widen the road. What do you think of the idea? This is what other children might think.

We won't have anywhere to play.

There will be a lot more traffic polluting the air.

Sometimes, huge areas of countryside are cleared in order to build roads and airports which make it easier for us to get around.

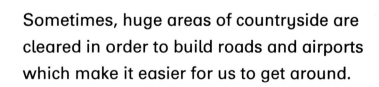

This forest in Brazil has been cleared to make way for a new road.

Explorers

Do you like going on journeys to explore new places? In the past, explorers went on long journeys to discover new countries and find out about the people that lived there. They travelled by sea, and it was often many months before they found land.

This picture shows the French arriving at Florida, on the west coast of America, in 1564.

Nowadays, we can travel around much more quickly and easily. Most parts of our Earth have already been explored. The only new places left to explore are the deep sea or very cold lands such as the Antarctic.

In October 1992, Sir Ranulph Fiennes and Michael Stroud spent 95 days crossing the Antarctic on foot.

If you were going to explore the Antarctic, what sort of things would you take with you? Here are some ideas.

gloves

tent

food and drink

skis

AX-21

The world of outer space is still a great mystery to us here on Earth. This is where tomorrow's explorers will go. Would you like to be one of them?

Index

For parents and teachers
More about the ideas in this book

Pages 6/7 Encourage the children to consider the needs of different journeys. Things to consider include the most appropriate form of transport, how much luggage is needed, what the weather will be like and what clothes to wear.

Pages 8/11 The reasons for making journeys may be pleasant or unpleasant, important or trivial. Journeys may take place on the spur of the moment or be planned well in advance. They may involve people or objects and take place every day, once in a while or once in a lifetime.

Pages 12/15 Methods of transport vary from place to place and country to country, depending on the landscape, the climate and the amount of public transport. The cost of different types of transport is also an important factor. Encourage the children to look for similarities and differences between transport in their local area and transport in other countries.

Pages 16/21 Maps can be used to trace the historical development of places and can be linked to maths activities on size and distance. Imaginary maps may develop through work on poems and stories.

Pages 22/23 Urban environments have a greater choice of roads and public transport but more traffic jams and pollution than rural places. Children could compare the variety and frequency of public transport in town and country areas.

Pages 24/25 The journeys we make cause a lot of damage to the environment. To minimise environmental problems we need to put money into public transport and more research time into pollution-free transport, such as solar-powered cars. Encourage the children to find out what other countries are doing to make journeys 'greener'.

Pages 26/27 In the past, explorers often exploited the lands and peoples they 'discovered'. Modern explorers are more aware of the rights of all people to live as they wish. Children could find out about organised expeditions such as those run by Operation Raleigh.

Things to do

Going places provides starting points for all kinds of cross-curricular work based on geography and the environment, both on a local and a global scale. **People on the move** explores the relationships between the journeys people make and land-use, landscape, transport and environmental issues. Here are some ideas for follow-up activities to extend the ideas further.

1 Draw maps of different journeys, such as a journey around a nature trail, a journey under the sea, a journey in a hot-air balloon, a journey to another planet, a journey to an imaginary island or the journey of a letter. Make a diary of the journey to record each stage in the right order.

2 Make a big scrapbook about different explorers past and present, such as Marco Polo, Columbus, Vasco da Gama, Hernan Cortez, Captain Cook, Captain Scott, Magellan, David Livingstone, Geoff Summers, Ranulph Fiennes, Wilfred Thesiger, Chris Bonington, Eric Newby and John Hillaby. Include some women explorers and travellers such as Clare Francis, Mary Kingsley and Christina Dodwell. How far did they travel? Why did they make their journeys? What did they discover? Did they change the places they visited?

3 Trace the history of one kind of transport and draw a time-line to show how much it has changed. What are the fastest forms of transport today? How safe are different forms of transport? What effect does transport have on the environment? Which is your favourite way to travel?

4 Plan an imaginary journey, perhaps a holiday, to find out about all the arrangements that need to be made. Look at timetables, tickets, passports, the weather, food to eat on the journey, clothes to take, games to play, places to stay and places to visit. Children could devise a checklist of things to take or a snakes-and-ladders board game of the journey.

5 Investigate the journeys made by settlers and refugees, such as the Pilgrim fathers, the Vietnamese boat people, Jews fleeing from the Nazis, Afro-Caribbean and Asian people who came to work in Britain in the 1950s or Greeks fleeing from Cyprus. Children could also plot the route to Australia taken by convict ships or the journeys of the slave trade.

6 People are not the only animals that go on journeys. Find out about bird migration. Birds migrate to find food, water or to avoid bad weather, but how do they find the way? How far do they fly? Do young birds follow the same routes as adults? Birds have to build up large fat reserves to sustain them on long flights. They can save energy by flying in V-formation and using thermals to glide over land.

7 Look at the history of road building. Why did the Romans build such good roads? In the Middle Ages, roads were dangerous places at night so people travelled by day. This is the origin of the word 'journey' which comes from the French word 'jour' and was originally used to mean 'a day's travel'. Famous road makers include Thomas Telford and John Macadam.

8 The word map comes from the Latin word 'mappa'. Map-making activities could include designing a maze (based on those in puzzle books or magazines), drawing a familiar object at different scales, drawing a treasure island map, designing a nature trail map and collecting different kinds of maps.